hinduism

A Brief Look at the Theology, Scriptures, and Social System, with Comments on the Gospel in India

hinduism

A Brief Look at the Theology,
Scriptures, and Social System,
with Comments on the Gospel in India

WILLIAM CAREY
LIBRARY

Book Design and Layout: Nigel Fernandes
Cover Design: Amanda Valloza
Cover Photograph: Miranda Stone,"Dawn on the Ghats of the Ganges River, Varanasi, India"

Published by William Carey Library
1605 E. Elizabeth Street, Pasadena, California 91104
www.missionbooks.org
William Carey Library is a ministry of the U.S. Center for World Mission, Pasadena, California.

Printed in the United States of America.

contents

introduction

About eighty percent of India's population is officially Hindu, as are most Indians scattered around the globe. Nepal until recently was an officially Hindu country and Pakistan, Bangladesh and Sri Lanka have smaller Hindu populations. Perhaps as many as ten percent of India's Hindus are better not considered Hindu, but rather followers of separate tribal religious traditions (the same is true for a still larger percentage of Nepal's population). This gives a world Hindu population in the area of 1 billion.

The followers of the Hindu religion are proud to point out that there is no single human founder and no known date of origin for Hinduism. The name Hinduism is, in fact, not rooted in India, but was born in efforts made by outsiders to define and understand the complex phenomena of religious life in India. In scholarly circles a great debate continues on what the word Hinduism really refers to, including suggestions that the term should never be used at all.

Hinduism is an evolved ensemble of faiths and practices, and the evolution has not by any means ceased. Hinduism today continues to change, most notably due to urbanization and globalization and in relation to the growth of militant politicized Hinduism. An understanding of the flow of Hindu history, including the development and themes of the scriptures of Hinduism, is essential for a balanced understanding. Yet historical understanding cannot be a substitute for knowing Hinduism as lived by adherents today. The diversity of Hindu beliefs and practices, however, makes a simple summary of practical Hinduism almost impossible.

The incredible diversity of ideas and rituals seen in Hinduism is a result of its growth over many centuries. The assimilative power of Hinduism has often been noted, and indeed Hinduism cannot be understood without clearly grasping this fact. Ideas that are totally contradictory are held by different sects and persons, yet all subsumed under the Hindu umbrella. Some pervasive practices, such as ancestor worship, are difficult to fit into any neat systematic theology.

Hindu history presents an array of brilliant systematic thinkers. The assimilation of new and foreign ideas, combined with the systematizing genius of brilliant leaders, is perhaps the greatest factor in the development of living Hinduism. It is of vital importance to note, however, that often the systematic summaries are rather artificial, and Hindu life continues with unresolved contradictions between sects that are oblivious to the neat patterns of the system makers.

This book will seek to balance the theoretical aspects of Hinduism with an understanding of its living practice. Salvation and the Hindu gods will first be considered, followed by the historical development and scriptures of Hinduism and then some comments on Hindu philosophy. Important themes related to the life of individuals and society will then be discussed. A final section will deal with the gospel of Christ in the Hindu world.

salvation and the gods of hinduism

The myth continues to be perpetrated that India is a land of spirituality and God-centeredness, while the West is dominated by materialism. That there is a great deal of truth to this generalization does not raise it from the realm of myth to that of fact.

Observers of Hindu practice have often pointed out that much of the devotion offered to various Hindu deities is with the rather unspiritual aim of obtaining worldly blessings, even to the point of crude bargaining. It must be noted that the formal teachings of Hinduism oppose this tendency, even as the Christian Scriptures speak against the gross materialism manifest in the lives of many Western Christians.

Salvation the goal of life

There are four guiding parameters for life in Hindu teaching. Pleasure (*kāma*) and productivity (*artha*) are esteemed, but are to be guided by *dharma* (righteous duty). Overriding all of these more earthly concerns is salvation (*moksha*), the supreme goal of life. Hindu teaching is thus holistic, touching into every area of life, yet keeps spiritual and eternal issues in the forefront. Within the diversity of Hinduism, however, there are strong disagreements even about what salvation itself means. It is generally agreed that humanity is trapped in a cycle of reincarnations, and salvation is escape from future rebirth in this world. But while what salvation is *from* might be agreed, what it is *to*, and *how it is achieved*, are by no means agreed. Traditionally, three paths to salvation are considered valid, and disputes as to which is the superior way have not been uncommon.

The way of knowledge

The way of knowledge (*jñāna mārga*) is proclaimed to be the highest by those who choose it. This is not rationalistic knowledge, however, but meditative supra-rational realization. In classical thought it is only through proper study and understanding of scripture (Veda) by a qualified (i.e. high caste) person that this can be achieved. Salvation in this understanding is moving beyond personality rather than an uplifting and purifying of the human personality.

The way of works

A second path is the way of works (*karma mārga*). At this point especially one must note the artificiality of this three-fold path summary. Virtually no one today is primarily following the way of works, and most Hindus demonstrate aspects of each of the three paths in their lives. Traditionally the works were mainly the sacrifices enjoined in the Vedic scriptures; in later developments all of one's duties in life were included, and today this is at times even redefined to include social service and humanitarian work.

The way of devotion

The third way of salvation, historically the last to come to prominence, is the way of devotion (*bhakti mārga*). This is by far the most popular path, to the point that this can be considered the essence of popular Hinduism (with care to remember that aspects of all three paths are evident in the lives of most Hindus). In the way of devotion one can choose the particular god on which to focus, and while most follow the traditional god or gods of their families, conversion from one god or guru to another is quite common. Salvation is to fellowship with and enjoyment of God, not to an emptiness beyond personality as in the way of knowledge.

God

Before explaining in some detail the gods to whom devotion is directed in hope of salvation, the general Hindu concept of God must be discussed. In the Indian languages there are numerous words that can be translated as "god," and the concept of God is accordingly complex. Efforts to briefly explain the Hindu concept of God are doomed to fail, simply because there is no one common concept. Some definitions that are commonly given can be mentioned in order to point out their inadequacy.

1. Hindus believe that God is ultimately impersonal. While this may be true for some Hindus (especially those following the *jñāna marga* [way of knowledge]), it is certainly not true for most.

2. Hindus are pantheists who believe everything is divine and thus anything can be worshipped. This is a complete misunderstanding of Hindu belief and practice.

3. Hindus are polytheists. In a sense, this is certainly true of most Hindus, yet as a blunt statement misses the subtlety of Hindu belief which consistently affirms faith in one God.

It is common to hear of the Hindu trinity (*trimurti*, which is really not comparable to the Christian trinity) of Brahma the creator, Vishnu the preserver, and Shiva the destroyer. This is a rather artificial alignment, however, and does not play an important role in the minds of most Hindus. As an alternative to these popular but misleading conceptions, Hinduism can better be considered as a group of religions gathered under one banner. These different "religions" subsumed under the Hindu umbrella have different theologies of God and affirm different gods as the supreme deity.

The Supreme Deity

Among the gods of Hinduism, considered to be 330 million in number, there are two different supreme deities; Vishnu, by far the most popular, and Shiva. Vaishnavism (Vishnu-ism) and Saivism (Shiva-ism) are far more truly two religions than Hinduism is one religion. The minority of Hindus who see God as ultimately impersonal and salvation as a transcending of personality can be viewed as yet another religion within the parameters of Hinduism. Systematizers have brought these divergent faiths together in various ways (such as the *trimurti*), but the distinctive theologies and rituals of the sects continue their strong hold over their adherents.

The boasted religious tolerance of the Hindus is manifest in the relationship between the followers of the supreme deities Vishnu and Shiva. Verbal duels between the groups have occurred, and at times even physical assaults. But in general there has been tolerance and mutual acceptance on the practical level while strong differences exist in beliefs.

Rather than condemning other gods, Hindus have traditionally assimilated them into lower levels of the hierarchy of spirits. So Shiva is considered a servant of Vishnu by those who consider Vishnu supreme, with the opposite relationship being believed by the followers of Shiva. This has obviously smoothed the way for popular worship of both, with the appearance of blatant polytheism. This appearance of polytheism is further enhanced by the large-scale worship of various goddesses. The Goddess in various manifestations is in fact a third major focus of worship beside Vishnu and Shiva. These three central figures and their worship must be further considered.

Vishnu

Vishnu (known also as Narayan and Hari among several other names) is the supreme God for most Hindus. Vaishnava mythology tells of

Vishnu lying in meditation in the primordial sea when a lotus blooms from his navel and Brahma, creator of our world, issues from the lotus. The devotees of Vishnu passionately believe in his *avatāras*, appearances on earth in human or even animal form. He is most popularly worshipped in either or both of his human *avatāras* as Ram and Krishna, represented by images of stone, metal, or clay, or in pictures. There are hundreds of sects of Vaishnavism with varying beliefs and practices.

Shiva

Shiva (also known as Mahesh, Mahadeva, Shankara, etc.) is the supreme God for many Hindus, especially in South India. While Vishnu as Ram and Krishna is worshipped with idols (often quite elaborately), Shiva is rather represented by a *linga* (with some exceptions as iconic forms of Shiva are not unknown), a simple emblem usually of stone that originally was a phallic symbol but which has lost this connotation among modern worshippers. One of the significant sects of modern Saivism, appropriately known as the Lingayats, are supposed to always wear a linga around their necks. Myths of Shiva portray him having children, one of whom is the elephant-headed god Ganesh (or Ganapati) whose image is widely worshipped since he is the remover of obstacles and so a god who smoothes the way to success.

The Goddess

The worship of God as mother or as female permeates most manifestations of Hinduism. The goddess is not usually seen as the supreme God, yet in various forms is represented as the consort of the major deities. As Durga and Kali (and others) she is associated with Shiva, as Lakshmi she is associated with Vishnu, etc. It must be noted as well that most villages maintain strong traditions of worship of the mother goddess, often involving animal sacrifice. The system linking these goddesses as consorts of the major gods often appears artificial.

The philosophy developed in the Tantras (more fully discussed later) makes the female the active power of the deity. Shakti (also at times spelled Sakti), which means power, is often used as a generic term for the goddesses, whose devotees are Shaktas. This theory that the true power lies with the goddess explains why so many Hindus turn to her (especially to Kali or Durga, the consort of Shiva) rather than to the so-called supreme God. There is, however, a developed theology of the goddess (usually Kali/Durga) as supreme deity, especially in Bengal in eastern India.

Conclusion

Vaishnavism, Saivism, and Shaktism have developed side by side in India, so it is understandable that there has been significant interchange of ideas and practices. The "average" Hindu would have a difficult time explaining with any coherency the multitudes of gods of Hinduism. But so would an "average" Christian make a mess of explaining the trinity!

The standard Hindu view of God is perhaps best described as a fluid monotheism. Vishnu has many manifestations, and who will dare to say what form God might not appear in? The Hindu is certain that God's ways are higher than ours, and so He is beyond our grasp. Jesus is easily accepted as a manifestation of God, as are various Muslim saints (despite the continued deep social tensions between the Hindu and Muslim communities in India), numerous Hindu gurus, and many mythological gods. The average Hindu is not concerned to reconcile the worship of many such figures with belief in one supreme God.

It should also be noted that Hinduism contains schools of thought that militantly oppose the idol worship (and guru worship) that accompanies popular Hindu devotion. There is also a philosophical position that grants the validity of idol worship as a lower form of devotion that more enlightened people move beyond. This latter position is popular among those with a Western education, but can hardly be considered *the* Hindu position. (On this point see also Chapter 4 on Hindu philosophy.)

In the midst of a practical polytheism, the foundational viewpoint of most Hindus is that there is a single supreme God who interacts with this world in various ways. It is to our advantage in this life to please God, and in God alone final salvation can be found.

the historical development of hinduism and the hindu scriptures

The oldest of the Hindu scriptures is the Rig Veda, a collection of over 1000 poems traditionally dated from around 1000 BC. Aryans migrated to the Indus River Valley (from which India got its name, though the river is now in Pakistan), bringing their faith in the various deities seen in the Rig Veda. The roots of what is now called Hinduism are traced to historical interaction between the Aryans and the ancient Indus Valley civilization.

The Rig Veda is the fountainhead of Hinduism and is appealed to as an authority by almost all Hindus. In practical terms, however, the Rig Veda has as little influence on Hindu life and thought today as the book of Leviticus has on Christians. Already in Vedic times and particularly in the post-Vedic period the developing history of Hinduism is the story of the interaction of Aryan and pre-Aryan Indian ideas and practices. Scholars have sought to sort out the various strands but the assimilation has been complete and there is no easy division.

A body of literature called Brāhmanas developed out of the Vedic hymns, followed by speculative discourses called Upanishads. (There can be no strict chronology here; the earliest hymns clearly predate the Brāhmanas, but there is overlapping regarding the later hymns.) The Brāhmanas were produced by priests (Brāhmans) and dealt mainly with elaborate details of prayers and rituals that the priests were to perform. The Upanishads are a collection of speculative poems of the utmost interest and importance. The concept of reincarnation, universal in later Indian thought, is developed here. The Upanishads continue to be read and studied by philosophically oriented Hindus.

The Upanishads prove that a powerful spiritual and philosophical movement developed in early India, roughly dated to the sixth and fifth centuries BC. Around that same time the profoundly important spiritual movements of Buddhism and Jainism arose. At times and in various places either Buddhism or Jainism were more powerful and popular than the various expressions of what is now called Hinduism. Over a period of many centuries these Hindu religious expressions, quite transformed in the process of interaction with Buddhism and Jainism, came to be the dominant religious factors in Indian life.

A significant body of legal and speculative literature was developed in the period following the Upanishads. The most widely known legal work is The Laws of Manu, but there were many other such important writings known as the Dharmasastras. The six schools of philosophy developed, in which the Brahma Sutras played a leading role. But it was the two great Hindu epics that captured the hearts of the common people. The Ramayana and the Mahabharata continue to have a powerful influence on the Hindu mind, not least through the long serialization of each on Indian television.

Two other bodies of literature, composed after Buddhism and Jainism had been largely vanquished in the early centuries of the Christian era, complete the scriptures of Hinduism in the Sanskrit language. The Puranas, of which there are reputed to be eighteen major books and at least another eighteen of lesser importance, are scriptures that continue to express and mold the faith of millions of Hindus. The Tantras were deeply influential in eastern India and have left an impact on virtually every aspect of Hindu life. These works appeared from the sixth to twelfth centuries AD.

The law books, epics, and Puranas are technically of lesser importance than the Vedic writings, but in practice the Hinduism of the masses is molded by these later writings. There is no commonly agreed upon definition of what is a scriptural book, however. Some Hindus look down on various of the Puranas and Tantras, and would never consider them in the same light as the Upanishads. The volume of writings that can be called scripture is not only overwhelming to the outsider; most Hindus are acquainted with only a small percentage of the books mentioned here.

Overlapping in date with the Puranic writings in Sanskrit there began to be deeply religious writing in the various vernacular languages of India. Tamil poems are the deepest scripture for many Hindus in the southern state of Tamil Nadu. The most important of all scriptures in Hindi-speaking north India is surely the Hindi adaptation of the Ramayana, written by Tulsidas in the sixteenth century AD. Writings of similar importance are found in the vernaculars of most of the linguistic regions of India, and can only be discounted as scripture if the opinion and practice of Hindus themselves are ignored.

Four Vedas

The Rig Veda is by far the most important of the four Vedas. The Sama and Yajur Vedas draw almost all their material from it. The fourth, the Atharva Veda, is generally accepted to be later in origin. It borrows about one sixth of its poems from the Rig Veda and contains many poems describing magical formulas and rituals.

The Rig Veda is neither a worship manual nor a philosophical treatise. It is a collection of poems directed to various deities, and the contents are often mundane at best. Flashes of brilliance appear, however, as well as seminal ideas that influenced the future development of Indian religious life.

No *mantra* (verse) of the Rig Veda is more widely known than that from Book 1, No. 144, verse 46: "They call him Indra, Mitra,

Varuna, Agni, and he is heavenly nobly-winged Garutman. To what is One, sages give many a title: they call it Agni, Yama, Matarisvan" (From *The Hymns of the Rgveda*, tr. R. T. H. Griffith, Motilal Banarsidass, New Delhi, rev. ed. 1973). The concept of "the One" behind many names and manifestations later developed into both monotheism and non-dualism (monism).

A number of creation hymns, considered among the last of the poems to be written, present the richest philosophical thought in the Rig Veda. The following from Book 10, Hymn Number 129, illustrates the depth and power of the speculative thought of the ancient *rishis*.

1. There was neither non-existence nor existence then;
    there was neither the realm of space nor the sky which is beyond.
    What stirred? Where? In whose protection?
    Was there water, bottomlessly deep?

2. There was neither death nor immortality then.
    There was no distinguishing sign of night nor of day.
    That one breathed, windless, by its own impulse.
    Other than that there was nothing beyond.

3. Darkness was hidden by darkness in the beginning;
    with no distinguishing sign, all this was water.
    The life force that was covered with emptiness,
    that one arose through the power of heat.

4. Desire came upon that one in the beginning;
    that was the first seed of mind.
    Poets seeking in their heart with wisdom
    found the bond of existence in non-existence.

5. Their cord was extended across.
    Was there below? Was there above?
    There were seed placers; there were powers.
    There was impulse beneath; there was giving-forth above.

6. Who really knows? Who will here proclaim it?
    Whence was it produced? Whence is this creation?

The gods came afterwards, with the creation of this universe.
Who then knows whence it has arisen?

7. Whence this creation has arisen—
   perhaps it formed itself, or perhaps it did not—
   the one who looks down on it, in the highest heaven,
   only he knows—
   or perhaps he does not know.

*(From The Rig Veda, W. D. O'Flaherty, Penguin Books,
London, 1981.)*

Upanishads

"Vedas" can refer to either the four collections of hymns, or to the
hymn collections and Brāhmanas and Upanishads together.
(Sometimes the Upanishads are seen as two parts, Aranyakas and
Upanishads, making four parts of the Vedas instead of the three
outlined here.) It is in the latter broad meaning that the Vedas are
the authoritative source books for Hinduism. In practical terms this
authority is in the Upanishads, the Brāhmanas being even
more neglected in modern Hinduism than the hymns. The
Upanishads are also called the Vedanta, which means the end or
goal of the Vedas.

The Upanishads develop and deepen the Rig Vedic theme of the
One behind the many manifestations of reality. This one is called,
in the Sanskrit language of the Vedas, *brahman* (or *brahma* or *brahm*;
the a's are all short). This *brahman* must not be confused with the
similar terms *brāhman* (the first a is long, meaning the priests, highest
of the caste groups, traditionally (and misleadingly) spelled in English
as Brahmin; the Brāhmanas are scriptures tied to the *brāhmans*) and
Brahmā (when the second a is long, this is the name of a particular
god, often referred to as the creator).

The philosophy of *brahman* is not consistently developed in the
various Upanishads, giving room for heated debate among the

various schools of Vedantic philosophy that later developed (and continue to today). (See further below in Chapter 4, Hindu Philosophy.) The most provocative of speculations on *brahman* conclude that the *ātman* is not different from *brahman* (*ātman* is generally defined as the human soul or spirit or self, but perhaps is better thought of as "God considered as immanent within the human person"). The Upanishads especially set the tone of high spirituality and mysticism that distinguish Hinduism in general.

Noteworthy *mantras* from the Upanishads

The priest whose function is to praise begins his praises with the Saman chant. When he begins his praises he should mutter these words:
From the unreal lead me to the real!
From darkness lead me to the light!
From death lead me to immortality!
(Brihadaranyaka Upanishad 1:3:28)

This Self—what can one say of it but 'No, No!'
It is impalpable, for it cannot be grasped;
indestructible, for it cannot be destroyed;
free from attachment, for it is not attached to anything, not bound.
It does not quaver nor can it be hurt.
(Brihadaranyaka Upanishad 3:9:26)

That which cannot be expressed by speech,
By which speech itself is uttered,
That is Brahman—know thou this—
Not that which is honoured here as such.

That which thinks not by the mind,
By which, they say, the mind is thought,
That is Brahman—know thou this—
Not that which is honoured here as such.

That which sees not by the eye,
by which the eyes have sight,
That is Brahman—know thou this—
Not that which is honoured here as such.

That which hears not by the ear,
By which this ear is heard,
That is Brahman—know thou this—
Not that which is honoured here as such.

That which breathes not by the breath,
By which breath is drawn in,
That is Brahman—know thou this—
Not that which is honoured here as such.

(Kena Upanishad 1:4-8)

The father: "Bring me a fig from over there."
The son, Svetaketu: "Here you are, sir."
"Cut it open."
"There it is, cut open, sir,"
"What do you see there?"
"These rather small seeds, sir."
"Would you, please, cut one of them up?"
"Here is one, cut up, sir."
"What do you see there?"
"Nothing at all, sir."
Then he said to him, "My dear boy, it is true that you cannot perceive this finest essence, but it is equally true that this huge fig tree grows up from this same finest essence.
"My dear child, have faith.
"This finest essence—the whole universe has it as its Self: That is the Real: That is the Self: That you are, Svetaketu!"

(Chandogya Upanishad 6:12:1-3)
(Upanishadic translations from R. C. Zaehner,
Hindu Scriptures, J. M. Dent & Sons, London, 1978.)

Sutras and Sastras

Between the Vedic period and up through the time of the growth of popular devotional literature there were prolific developments expressed in various scriptures that today are much more for scholars than practitioners.

Sutras, among which the Brahma Sutras (also referred to as the Vedanta Sutras) holds pride of place for its role in Hindu philosophy (Vedanta), are cryptic mnemonic devices that are almost indecipherable without exposition from one clued in to the meaning. Three broad classes of sutra literature are the Srautasutras (aphorisms regarding ritual), the Grihyasutras (aphorisms on family duties) and the Dharmasutras (aphorisms on religious duties).

Sastras are a broad set of works touching on many topics, most noteworthy being the Dharmasastras or treatises on religious duties, of which the Laws of Manu is the most familiar.

The opening aphorisms of the Brahma Sutras

1. Then therefore the enquiry into *brahman*.
2. (*Brahman* is that) from which the origin, etc. (i.e. the origin, subsistence and dissolution) of this (world proceed).

(From The Vedanta Sutras with the Commentary of
Sankarakarya, tr. George Thibaut,
vol. 34 of The Sacred Books of the East,
ed. F. Max Muller; The Clarendon Press, Oxford, 1890)

Ramayana

The original Ramayana, attributed to Valmiki, was written in Sanskrit perhaps as early as the third century BC. It has been rewritten with large scale adaptation into numerous vernacular languages. It is not fully valid to speak of the Ramayana as one book due to the variations in these different Ramayanas. There is, however, an unchanging core of the story.

The Ramayana is a truly epic account of events in the life of noble king Ram (or Rama) and his faithful wife Sita. Due to palace intrigues, Ram is unjustly banished from his kingdom for fourteen years. The embodiment of peace and tranquility, Ram submits to the injustice. Sita insists on following her husband into exile and faces unspeakable hardships.

While in exile, the faithful Sita is abducted by evil king Ravana. Ram and his cohorts, most notably Hanuman, finally achieve the rescue of Sita, whose conduct under captivity was impeccable. Ram and Sita are restored to their rightful kingdom to the acclaim of all their subjects.

How much of a historical core lies behind the Ramayana is a widely debated issue. In Valmiki's original Sanskrit edition Ram is often clearly a human figure. By later editions, notably Tulsidas' sixteenth century AD Hindi work, Ram is the highest divinity of all, through whom alone salvation can be found. In its various formats the Ramayana upholds a high ideal of conduct. Especially Sita is upheld to women as the most noble example of feminine virtue, whom all should emulate.

Statements from the Ramayana of Tulsidas

> Let them preach in their wisdom, who contemplate thee as Supreme Spirit, the Uncreated, the inseparable from the universe, recognizable only by inference and beyond the understanding; but we, O Lord, will unceasingly hymn the glories of thy incarnation. O merciful Lord, home of compassion, this is the boon we ask, that in thought, word, and deed, and without any variableness we may maintain a devotion to thy feet. (VII, Chand 5)

> ...I have sung to the best of my ability his holy and gracious deeds. In this, the last age of the world, there is no other means of salvation, neither abstraction, sacrifice, prayer, penance, the paying of vows, nor religious ceremonial. Meditate only on Rama, sing only of Rama, give ear only to Rama's infinite perfections. Let the soul

give over its perversity and worship him whose special characteristic it is to sanctify the fallen, as is declared by saints and seers, by Veda and Puranas: is there anyone who has worshipped Rama and not found salvation?

(VII, Caupai 125, The Ramayana of Tulsidas; Growse, F. S., rev. ed. Motilal Banarsidass, New Delhi, 1978)

Mahabharata

The Mahabharata is clearly not the work of one person, but more like an encyclopedia with contributions on a wide range of subjects from a wide range of people over a significant period of time. It is the longest epic poem in the world, with 110,000 couplets. Parts seem clearly to pre-date the Ramayana, while much is also clearly composed later than the Ramayana.

The basic story line is of a great war, yet this accounts for only about a quarter of the epic. The battle of Kurukshetra is fought between cousins. The Pandavas finally prevail over the Kauravas, and Yudhistir, eldest of the Pandavas, is enthroned as king. Yudhistir later renounces the throne, goes on pilgrimage, and is received into heaven.

Various digressions covering a wide range of themes make up the largest part of the Mahabharata. The most famous of these digressions from the war story is the brilliant philosophical exposition known as the Bhagavad Gita.

Bhagavad Gita

The Bhagavad Gita ("Song of the Blessed Lord") is often printed as a separate book, yet is also one section of the great Mahabharata epic. Technically the Gita is not a Vedic scripture, so is not of the highest authority. Traditionally, however, it is accepted as a systematic summation of all that is best in the Vedic literature. In practice it is the central Scripture for understanding the rudiments of Hindu philosophy.

The setting of the Bhagavad Gita is a war between two sections of a family. Arjuna, of the Pandava clan, shrinks from fighting, knowing the horrors of death and destruction that are inevitable. He is urged to get on and fight by his charioteer, who is no less than the divine Krishna. Using such an unlikely setting on a field of battle, the unknown author of the Gita presents his teaching.

The doctrine of *avatāras*, God's descending and appearing as a man, is central to the Gita's teaching. The human race is to respond to God with love and devotion. Hundreds of commentaries have been written on the Gita, and various schools of Hindu thought have their distinctive interpretations.

Selections from the Gita

The Blessed Lord [Krishna] said:
Many a birth have I passed through,
And many a birth hast thou:
I know them all,
Thou knowest not.

Unborn am I, changeless is my Self;
Of all contingent beings I am the Lord!
Yet by my creative energy (*māyā*) I consort
With Nature—which is mine—and come to be in time.

For whenever the law of righteousness
Withers away, and lawlessness
Raises its head
Then do I generate Myself on earth.

For the protection of the good,
For the destruction of evildoers,
For the setting up of righteousness,
I come into being, age after age.

(Bhagavad Gita 4:5-8)

In the region of the heart of all
Contingent beings dwells the Lord,

Twirling them hither and thither by his uncanny power
   (*māyā*)
Like puppets fixed in a machine.

In Him alone seek refuge
With all thy being, all thy love;
And by his grace shalt thou attain
An eternal state, the all-highest peace.

Of all mysteries most mysterious
This wisdom have I told thee;
Ponder on it in all its amplitude,
Then do whatever thou wilt.

And now again give ear to this my all-highest Word,
Of all the most mysterious:
'I love thee well'
Therefore will I tell thee thy salvation.

Bear me in mind, love me and worship me,
Sacrifice, prostrate thyself to Me:
So shalt thou come to Me, I promise thee
Truly, for thou art dear to Me.

Give up all things of law,
Turn to Me, thine only refuge,
For I will deliver thee
From all evils; have no care.

Never must thou tell this to one
Whose life is not austere, to one devoid of love and loyalty,
To one who refuses to obey,
Or one who envies Me.

But whoever shall proclaim this all-highest mystery
To my loving devotees,
Showing the while the highest love and loyalty to Me,
Shall come to Me in very truth.

(Bhagavad Gita 18:61-68)
(Gita translations from R. C. Zaehner, Hindu Scriptures, op. cit.)

Puranas

The eighteen great and many lesser Puranas present stories of the creation, destruction and re-creation of the universe, genealogies of the gods, and tales from human history. The name *purāna* means "old" or "ancient," and many of the myths clearly have been passed down for many generations, often being transformed in the process, before they were written. Pride of place among the Puranas must go to the Bhagavata (also called Srimad Bhagavatam).

The Bhagavata Purana relates the story of the many *avatāras* (descents, or in Christian terms "manifestations in history") of God (Vishnu). "O Saints! Innumerable are the incarnations (*avatāras*) of the Lord," states chapter three of book one. But especially twenty-two incarnations are noted. In popular piety the twenty-two are usually reduced to ten, often represented in sculpture and alluded to in poetry.

The outstanding section of the Bhagavata Purana, widely translated and loved, is chapter ten. This is the story of Krishna, the naughty child who is almighty Lord and the young man who sports with the girls and wives of the neighborhood. The latter sexual analogy of the divine-human relation plays no small role in various aspects of Hinduism. Though it is explained philosophically, it cannot be considered to have always had an ennobling influence, and at times led to shameful acts as in some schools of Tantrism (see below on the Tantras).

From the Bhagavata Purana

One day when Balarama and other sons of the cow-herds were playing together, they coming to mother Yashoda said unto her, 'Krishna hath eaten earth.' Thereupon Yashoda being desirous of his welfare, holding Krishna by the hand, reprimanded him. At this Krishna's eyes indicated fear, and Yashoda spoke thus unto him—'O you naughty boy, why have you eaten earth in secret? These boys, your companions and your elder brother are speaking to that effect.' 'Oh no mother, I have not eaten it; they are all liars. If you think they are truthful, you may examine my mouth.'

Yashoda said, 'Very well, then open your mouth.' After having thus been spoken to, the Almighty Hari [Vishnu] (in the present form of Krishna) of unimpeded prosperity, who had in his sport assumed the form of a human child, opened his mouth. Yashoda then saw inside the mouth of Krishna, the whole universe, the mobile and immobile creation, the ethereal dome, the heavenly quarters, the grand divisions of the earth with the mountains, the oceans and the mundane sphere, the atmosphere, the fire and lightening, the Zodiac with the moon and the stars, water, light, the sky, the deities presiding over the senses, the sense organs, the mind, the objects of perception, and the three Principles. She saw in the person of her son, inside his gaping mouth, the vast and grand universe in its entirety filled with different structures created by soul, the time, nature, actions, and desires; as also the kingdom of Braj with her own self.

(10:8:32-39, quoted from The Srimad Bhagavatam, trans. J. M. Sanyal, Munshiram Manoharlal, New Delhi, 1973.)

Tantras

The Tantras, the primary scriptures of Shaktism or Tantrism, are among the last of the Sanskrit scriptures. They have often been considered an expression of a degenerate form of Hinduism. This is not entirely fair, however, especially since there are two major sections of Tantric (Shakta) belief and practice.

Right-handed Tantrism is popular Hinduism with devotion centered on the goddess (see the last poem under Vernacular Poets below, for example). Left-handed Tantrism involved (the past tense is not fully accurate, as no doubt such rites continue today in secret practice, but not widely) sexual rituals and human sacrifice. The latter has been widely opposed and many of the writings of these sects were destroyed by both Hindus and Muslims.

To consider the extremes of left-handed Tantric practice as a true and natural fruit of Hinduism is like considering World Wars I and II to be the fruit of Christianity.

The concept of Kundalini Yoga, propagated by some aspects of the New Age Movement, is Tantric in origin. Although the Tantric scriptures are late, there is reason to believe that the roots of Tantrism are deep in the history of Hinduism and of India. Worship of the mother goddess, which touches the essence of Tantrism, can be traced to the Indus Valley civilization, perhaps pre-dating the Rig Veda. It has already been noted that Tantric influences (goddess worship and animal sacrifice) are widely manifest in popular Hinduism.

Vernacular Poets

The later Sanskrit scriptures were composed when vernacular languages were developing, and in time these vernaculars became the dominant means of religious expression. Tamil is an ancient language, and collections of Tamil poetry are the true scriptures for many Hindus in the southern state of Tamil Nadu. Collections of vernacular religious poetry and songs (along with translations of Sanskrit scriptures) are found in most modern Indian languages, and some of these are undoubtedly to be reckoned among the scriptures of Hinduism.

The first great school of vernacular *bhakti* (devotional) poets arose in the southern Tamil region around the seventh century AD. There is debate as to whether or not there may have been some small degree of Christian influence on this movement. This devotional movement spread slowly to the north, where it thrived in the fifteenth and following centuries. There was definite Islamic influence on aspects of the north Indian movement.

The *bhakti* movements flourished under the charismatic influence of gifted poets and singers. In South India there were two branches, one which directed devotion to Shiva, and the other to Vishnu. In North India the movement was more strongly Vaishnavite, but also contained a non-sectarian element, part of which developed into the new religion of Sikhism under Guru Nanak (1469-1533) and his successors.

Some themes in the *bhakti* poets are closely in line with biblical teaching, although in other topics the differences remain great. There is often a strong criticism of idolatry and caste, yet there has been little practical outworking of this teaching of these brilliant poets.

Selections from the bhakti *poets*

> Why fast and starve, why suffer pains austere?
> Why climb the mountains, doing penance harsh?
> Why go to bathe in waters far and near?
> Release is theirs, and theirs alone, who call
> At every time upon the Lord of all.
>
> *(Apparswami (eighth century AD?), trans. from Tamil, from Hymns of the Tamil Saivite Saints, F. Kingsbury and G. E. Phillips, Association Press, Calcutta, 1921, pg 57.)*

> The waking sleep and the sleepers sleep till God's mercy
>   they discern;
> The waking wake and the sleepers wake when His blessed
>   name they learn.
> They that see are blind and the blind are blind until the
>   truth is known;
> They that see behold and the blind behold when they
>   make God's love their own.
> They that speak are dumb and the dumb are dumb till the
>   secret comes abroad;
> The speakers speak and the dumb too speak when they lift
>   their hearts to God.

They that live are dead and the dead are dead till they
   behold His face;
The living live and the dead too live in God their
   Dwelling Place.

(Song 307 of Dadu Dayal (1544-1603),
trans. from Hindi, from A Sixteenth Century Indian Mystic,
W. G. Orr, Lutterworth Press, London, 1947, title page.)

I am a mass of sin;
   Thou art all purity;
Yet thou must take me as I am
   And bear my load for me.

Me Death has all consumed
   In thee all power abides.
All else forsaking, at thy feet
   Thy servant Tuka hides.

(by Tukaram (1608-1649), trans. from Marathi,
from Psalms of Maratha Saints, Nicol Macnicol,
Association Press, Calcutta, 1919, pg 65.)

Herald of Death, get hence! I am the son of the Almighty
Mother. Go, ask your Master how many like me he has seized.
I can be the death of Death, if I remember the Almighty
Mother's power.

Prasad says: Herald of Death, take heed what you say to me!
Fellow, in Kali's name I will bind you; and when I smite you,
who will save?

(by Ramprasad Sen (1718-1775), trans. from Bengali,
from Bengali Religious Lyrics, Sakta, Edward J. Thompson,
Association Press, Calcutta, 1923, pg 65.)

four

hindu philosophy

distinctions between religion and philosophy, and particularly between theology and philosophy, can be difficult to define, and often there is the impression that "philosophy" is promoted by those with an elitist disdain for "doctrine." The agenda for discussions of Hindu issues is still dominated by the work of nineteenth century Orientalists who especially had a bias against religion and promoted philosophy as a superior discipline.

Neat and rather artificial systems related to Hindu philosophy have developed, particularly the popular teaching about six "orthodox" schools of Hindu philosophy, beside which there are numerous "unbelieving" philosophies. Yet there is no true standard for "orthodoxy" in Hindu systems, and the differences among the so-called orthodox schools can be quite monumental. Among the so-called unbelieving schools of thought are ancient hedonists, Buddhists, and (in the popular denunciations common in theological debate) even at times some of the orthodox schools, such as Yoga which denies the existence of a supreme deity.

The dominant school of Hindu philosophy has long been Vedanta, also at times referred to as Uttara Mimamsa. Aspects of the thought of the other orthodox schools continue to be influential but will not be noted here. Vedantic thought, based on the Upanishads, Bhagavad Gita, and Brahma Sutras, is too important to bypass.

Vedanta philosophy is often mistakenly spoken of as a unity, when in fact there are various schools of Vedantic thought. There is no more serious, nor perhaps more common, error in the study of Hinduism than the error of considering Advaita Vedanta as if this *is* Hindu philosophy.

Advaita

Advaita Vedanta is unquestionably one of the greatest and noblest of all the world's philosophical systems. Its classical exposition was by Shankara in the eighth to ninth century AD. Advaita means "not-two," "non-dual," and seeks to explain the *brahman* of the Upanishads as the only true reality beside which all that is seen as reality is truly nothing (*māyā*, generally defined as illusion). This *brahman* cannot be conceived of as personal since it is beyond all conceiving. Relatively few Hindus are true advaitins, yet the influence of this system is far reaching, touching into virtually every aspect of Hindu thought and practice. It is a powerful influence in the New Age Movement which is now popular in the Western world.

Vishishtadvaita

Vishishtadvaita, qualified non-dualism, is far more truly the philosophy of most Hindus. Ramanuja is the great eleventh century AD philosopher who propagated this with virulent attacks on Shankara's advaita. Ramanuja's is a more theistic position, defining the goal of salvation as fellowship with and enjoyment of God (this is the prime philosophical position for the *bhakti* [devotional] path to salvation). It should be noted that Ramanuja's theism differs from traditional Christian theism primarily in that the created world is seen as an emanation out of God rather than a true creation by God out of nothing.

Neo-advaita of Vivekananda

Still other Vedantic schools could be considered, but what is now known as neo-advaita, or even neo-Hinduism, cannot be passed over. Swami Vivekananda (1863-1902) can be considered the founder of the new advaita, which is a missionary religion claiming to have the solutions to all of life's problems. Vivekananda propagated the idea that all religions are basically valid, while also clearly defining higher and lower forms.

Advaita, in which God transcends personality and morality, is considered by Vivekananda as the highest form of religion or philosophy. Polytheism and idolatry are low forms, but valid enough for those who cannot rise above them. Focus on a personal God or manifestation of God, such as Jesus, is perfectly good for those who choose it, but of course not as good as advaita which is destined to prove superior in the long run. Christian emphasis on sin is an insult to human nature, which is truly divine. These and similar neo-advaitic ideas hardly sum up the faith of Hinduism, but have become common currency among Westernized sections of Hindus and often are presented to the West as the true face of Hinduism. Even people who do not deeply believe these ideas will often quote them to Christians, since this school of thought has been most vigorous in defense against and attack on Christianity.

five

aspects of individual and social life in hinduism

Caste

One of the names for Hinduism commonly used by Hindus is *varnāshram dharma*, which can be paraphrased as "duty [to God] according to caste and stage of life." Caste, *varna* or *jāti*, may be defined easily in theory but it is impossible to systematize what it is in practice. In theory there are four major caste (*varna*) groups, with a large group remaining outside these four.

The Brahman or priestly caste is generally acknowledged as highest, although the Kshatriya or warrior/ruler caste has at times disputed this. The third caste of Vaisya is the business caste and the fourth, the Sudra, is the manual laborers. In fact, this traditional occupational division does not hold true as numerous individuals work outside the sphere of their caste's designated role.

In practice, *jāti* (which is really a different concept from that of *varna*, but "caste" is the only English equivalent for either term) is the important concept. There are many varieties of Brahman *jāti*, and they contest among themselves which type of Brahman is higher and which is lower. The Vaisya caste is harder to define and really does not properly exist in some areas of India. The Sudra caste, which would be massive in number (more than the three higher castes combined), is not a living and relevant concept in much of modern India. Technically the Sudras are unclean and cannot be taught the Vedic scriptures. In practice, in some places there are clean Sudra groups distinguished from unclean Sudras.

The government of India now speaks of Other Backward Castes, which basically refers to the Sudras. The "other" is in comparison to the so-called outcastes, referred to politically as Scheduled Castes due to a schedule (list) of castes granted special privileges due to their traditionally backward status. Among the "outcastes," now generally being referred to as Dalits (from a Sanskrit word meaning "oppressed"), there are caste (*jāti*) divisions and rivalries that parallel those among the Brahmans! The population of the many Dalit castes is virtually equal to that of the three high castes combined.

In summary, there are three broad groups within the caste structure. The three high castes are socially and culturally similar, with a significant gap between them and the Other Backward Castes (roughly equivalent to the Sudras). The Other Backward Castes generally demonstrate a similar superior attitude towards the Scheduled Castes (outcastes, Dalits), with an accompanying social and cultural gap. Christianity in India has only penetrated a limited number of Scheduled Caste groups, with all of the higher Hindu groups unresponsive to the gospel of Christ.

Discrimination on the basis of caste is now outlawed in India, and modernization is breaking down numerous caste taboos. From the lowest Dalit castes individuals have risen to high positions in business and government, including the office of president of India (not yet prime minister, where the real political power lies). Despite reforms and progressive laws it is still generally true that the lower castes are backward and many individuals are doomed to a life without hope of improvement. India is still deeply fragmented on caste lines, and the disappearance of caste cannot be imagined in the near future.

Stages of life

Traditional teaching indicates that a person must work in accordance with his caste, as also with his stage of life (*āshram*). The first stage of life is that of the student, initiated among the three high castes by a ceremony in which a sacred thread is draped over the neck and one shoulder. The thread is now mostly worn only by Brahmans, and not even by all Brahmans. (Sudras, outcastes, and women did not receive the thread, nor the Vedic education that was begun with the thread ceremony.)

The second stage of life is that of the householder. Hindus highly esteem family life, and the strength of Hinduism has traditionally been the home. Daily worship of God or gods is a standard part of home life. Most of the sacraments of Hinduism (naming of a child, the thread ceremony, marriages, funerals, etc.) are practiced in the home with a designated priest performing the ceremony.

When a man has raised his family (the role of women in traditional Hinduism is often ambivalent at best) he is enjoined to retreat from the busyness of life and spend time in contemplation and meditation in a quiet place. This third *āshram* (stage of life) relates closely to the more commonly known meaning of ashram as a place for quiet retreat.

After time in contemplation and meditation a fourth stage of life is that of the homeless wanderer, or *sannyāsi*. In practice, Hinduism has long allowed for men at any stage of life, and for women, to become sadhus or sannyasis. There is no doubt that many sincere spiritual men and women, as well as some diabolical imposters, have been and are numbered among these holy men and women.

Renunciation

Renunciation, most clearly demonstrated by the sadhus and sannyasis, is a value highly esteemed by Hindus. Fasting is commonly practiced by most devout Hindus. The close relationship in Hindu thinking between spirituality and simplicity/renunciation, which is not an anti-biblical thought, raises many questions about the possibility of true spirituality even existing in materialistic cultures. The last stage of life, involving the renunciation of this world in preparation for and witness to eternity, deeply impacts Hindu thinking.

There is nobility and profound practicality in this four-fold scheme of life, yet this has rarely been practiced anywhere nearly as neatly as it can be defined. But Hindu teaching is clear that the duty of a military family man will be quite different from the duty of a student or of a retired priest. There is a common ethical core to Hindu teaching on life, perhaps most notably in the Bhagavad Gita's call to serve without desire for reward (*nishkāma karma*). But what exactly the service entails depends on one's caste (occupation) and stage of life.

Holy times and places

The life of the average Hindu will only be misunderstood if a large place is not given to the concept of auspicious times and places. Hinduism follows a lunar calendar (many different calendars in different regions of India), and one half of each month when the moon is waxing is auspicious, while the other half when the moon is waning is inauspicious. This is only a first principle of a complex system of establishing auspicious and inauspicious times. Astrological prognostications are central to the lives of many Hindus, and are considered essential by most when deciding on the date for a wedding or other important event.

Holy places are also of vital importance. With modern means of transportation pilgrimage as a mixed holiday and spiritual adventure is prevalent to a higher degree than ever before in the history of India. Pilgrimage sites are often places of exceptional natural beauty, celebrated for the historical presence of a revered figure from the past or by a mythological story of the acts of a god.

Local temples also often have a history or myth behind their location. While the Hindu home must be counted more significant than the temple, temple worship is nevertheless a vital aspect of Hindu life. It has often been pointed out that temple worship is not usually congregational in the way that Christian worship is, but rather individual in a central location. Simultaneous worship directed at the image (or linga in a Shiva temple) by numerous individuals in different stages of their devotional ritual creates an atmosphere that seems chaotic to the outside observer.

Festivals

Religious ceremonies and festivals are celebrated at the most auspicious times (and also at the inauspicious times, for obvious reasons). Often the holy times and places come together, as at the great Kumbha Mela held every twelve years in Allahabad in north India where the great rivers Ganges and Yamuna meet. There are a few major all-India festivals, numerous large festivals of importance in one region or other, and innumerable other festivals of decreasing geographical importance down to the small local temples.

Some of the most important festivals and their significance must be noted. Dassera begins the longest annual festival season, just after the monsoons. This begins as Navaratri ("nine nights") or Durga-puja, a celebration of the goddess' victory over a great demon. The tenth day marks the celebration of Ram's victory over Ravana (as in the Ramayana epic). In north India a larger Ram festival overlaps and at times overshadows the goddess' festival.

Divali (or Deepavali) follows some weeks later and lasts five days. This is the festival of lights when homes and temples are illumined, as are many roads and riversides. Many relate this to an annual visit of Lakshmi, goddess of wealth and good fortune, whereas others commemorate in it the triumphant return and enthronement of Ram with Sita (Ramayana epic).

Shivaratri ("Shiva's night") and Krishnajayanti (Krishna's birthday) are of all-Indian importance. Pongal is a major three day festival in south India, rather like a thanksgiving service and celebration of the goodness of life. Holi is mainly north Indian, a carnival involving the spraying of colors on people's clothing and loud processions, sometimes accompanied by immoral taunting, in a paradoxical reversal of norms. Hinduism without festivals is unimaginable.

The fact that India today still has a large population of illiterates, and a vastly higher percentage of such in previous generations, points to the importance of religious rituals and festivals in maintaining and developing the faith of Hindus. Communication by traditional modes of song, drama, dance, narration, etc., mark all the festivals. Traditional communication techniques continue to rival and surpass the effectiveness of modern technological means. Many Hindus are now fusing modern and traditional devices with powerful effectiveness.

six

biblical witness to hindus

*W*hen Roman Catholic missionaries began work in India in the sixteenth century there was already a Christian church in the southern area that is now the state of Kerala. Sadly, this church had lost its spiritual vitality and any vision it might once have had for sharing its faith.

Roman Catholic missionaries, like the Protestants to follow, found responsive peoples among the lowest castes. Some work was done among the more orthodox and educated Hindus, most notably by the great Robert de Nobili. But no significant fruit ever followed from work among the higher castes.

Protestant missions began with German missionaries arriving in south India in 1706. A larger influx began with the arrival of William Carey in north India in 1793. The need and responsiveness of the lowest castes tended to overshadow a stated concern to reach the high castes. The great work of educational missions was successful in winning some high caste individuals to Christ, but never to the extent that missionaries expected.

The lower caste people who came to Christ usually came in great numbers over a period of a decade or two, a phenomenon widely studied under the name "people movements". In most cases these movements were inadequately followed up, the numbers being of

Some pointers for personal evangelism among Hindus

Friendship will almost always be welcomed by an Indian in the West. India is a relationally oriented society, and the time and business orientation of the West makes for a difficult adjustment. There may be an initial note of suspicion, since not too many Westerners offer their friendship; don't make the mistake of having an "agenda" that is more important than the person.

Your ignorance of Hinduism can be a help rather than a liability. Most Hindus esteem religion in general and are free and open to speak about it. A sincere, non-judgmental interest in all aspects of Indian life will provide a good basis for friendship. Personal interaction with Hindus will lead to a more certain grasp of the essence of Hinduism than the reading of many books can provide.

A consistently Christ-like life is the most important factor in sharing the gospel with Hindus. The suggestions that follow should help to break down misunderstandings, of which there are far too many, and help to build a positive witness for Christ. Yet learning and applying these points can never substitute for a transparent life of peace and joy in discipleship to Jesus Christ.

Dangers to avoid

1. *Do not criticize or condemn Hinduism.* There is much that is good and much that is bad in the practice of both Christianity and Hinduism. Pointing out the worst aspects of Hinduism is hardly the way to win friends or show love! It is to the credit of Hindus that they rarely retaliate against Christians by pointing out all our shameful practices and failures. Criticizing Hinduism can make us feel we have won an argument; it will not win Hindus to Jesus Christ.

2. *Do not argue or debate on points where we must disagree with our Hindu friends.* Most Hindus hold loosely their theology or philosophy. God is above our definitions and debates, and the

such magnitude and the needs being so great. No similar movement ever happened among the higher castes.

The work of missions in the twentieth century is more the story of the handing over of affairs from foreigners to Indians and the uniting of various denominations than of evangelization. There exists in India today a sizable church (roughly four percent of the population), and from that church there is a significant missionary movement. This missionary movement is largely aimed at the semi-Hindu tribal peoples of India, and also at the lowest castes, which remain responsive.

Despite the outstanding work of numerous missionaries and Indian Christians, meaningful communication of Jesus Christ to high caste Hindus is mostly noteworthy for its absence. Among the lower castes more has been and is being done, but nothing comparable to the magnitude of the spiritual and material need. The Hindu world consists of thousands of distinct caste/cultural people groups that remain largely without any witness to the reality and power of Christ. This blunt analysis is not to denigrate the ministry of Christian radio and of literature distribution, which have surely contributed to a greater understanding of Christ as well as leading some individuals to faith. But there is no room for complacency or facile optimism when the situation is truly surveyed.

Already during British rule there was a substantial movement of Hindus out of India to work in other parts of the world. In the last decades of the twentieth century a new exodus began, and Hindus are now living all across the globe, often in suburban neighborhoods in close proximity to churches. But "church" is understood as part of an alien civilization that is undermining many of the basic spiritual and familial values of Hindu civilization, and few Hindus will listen to a message coming from a church. Individual disciples of Christ need to make an effort to befriend Hindus if the gospel is ever to become meaningful in the Hindu world.

man of God should stand above human disagreements. Often points are raised to deflect a conversation from Christ and his compelling demands; keep a focus on Him and avoid debate.

3. *Never allow a suggestion that separation from family and/or culture is necessary in becoming a disciple of Christ.* To insist or even subtly encourage a Hindu to leave his home and way of life to join the "Christian" way of life in terms of diet and culture, etc. is a denial of Biblical teaching (see 1 Cor. 7: 17-24).

4. *Avoid all that even hints at triumphalism and pride.* We are not the greatest people with the greatest religion, but some Hindus are taught that we think of ourselves in this way. We do not have all knowledge of all truth; in fact we know very little (1 Cor. 8:1, 2). We do not desire all India to become Christian (think of what that means to a Hindu...India like America or Europe!)...but we do desire all India to find peace and joy and true spirituality. Be careful in using testimonies of Hindus who have found Christ, since triumphalism is often communicated and offends Hindus. Testimonies must be given with evident humility, and with love and esteem for Hindus and Hinduism.

5. *Do not speak quickly on Hell, or on the fact that Jesus is the only way for salvation.* Hindus regard these things as triumphalism and are offended unnecessarily. Speak of Hell only with tears of compassion. Point to Jesus so that it is obvious He is the only way, but leave the Hindu to see and conclude this for himself rather than trying to impose it on him.

6. *Never hurry.* Any pushing for a decision or conversion will do great harm. God must work, and the Holy Spirit should be given freedom to move at His own pace. Even after a profession of Christ is made, do not force quick changes regarding pictures of gods, charms, etc. Be patient and let a person come to full conviction in his own mind before taking action.

7. *Be careful when seeking biblical teachings in Hindu scriptures.* Scrupulous honesty is needed in interpreting the scriptures of

all religions, and one must diligently study the larger context of all quotations. There are, in fact, abundant points of contact between the Bible and Hindu scriptures on broad thematic issues, but claiming references to Christ where none exist only undermines credibility.

8. *There must be no sectarian denominational appeal.* Denominationalism is deadly and pushing small doctrines will stunt growth and offend spiritual seekers.

9. *There must be no pretense or pretending.* The suggestions made here must be honestly applied and fully embraced from the heart. To take these ideas merely as a strategy in evangelism but ignore them in the rest of our life and thinking would be a sin against God and could lead to nothing good.

Strengths to develop

1. *Work into your life the traditional Hindu (and Biblical!) values* of simplicity, renunciation, spirituality, and humility, against which there is no law. A life reflecting the reality of "a still and quiet soul" (Psalm 131) will never be despised by Hindus.

2. *Empathize with Hindus.* Appreciate all that is good and be truly sad about error and sin (as sad as you are about error and sin in Christianity). Learn to think as the Hindu thinks, and feel as he feels.

3. *Know Hinduism, and each individual Hindu.* It will take some study to get a broad grasp of Hinduism, and patient listening will be required to understand where in the spectrum each Hindu stands. Both philosophical and devotional Hinduism should be studied with the aim of understanding what appeals to the Hindu heart. Those who move towards serious incarnational ministry among Hindus need to become more knowledgeable in Hinduism than most Hindus themselves are. Some study of the Sanskrit language will prove invaluable. Remember the Biblical pattern from Acts 17 of introducing

truth to the Hindu from his own tradition, and only secondarily from the Bible. For example, the Biblical teaching on sin is repulsive to many modern Hindus, but their own scriptures give an abundance of similar testimony.

4. *Be quick to acknowledge failure.* Defending wrong practices in the church and Western Christianity only indicates we are more concerned about our religion than we are about the truth.

5. *Center on Christ.* He only can win the hearts of Hindus to total loyalty to Himself. In your life and speech so center on Him that all see in your life that God alone is worth living for. Hinduism is often called "God-intoxicated", and the Hindu who lives at all in this frame of mind is put off by Christian emphases on so many details to the neglect of the "one thing that is needed" (Lk. 10:42).

6. *Be quick to acknowledge mystery and lack of full understanding.* The greatest of thinkers know almost nothing about God, and the Hindu appreciates those who have a deep sense of the mystery of God and life. Don't pretend you understand and can explain Jn. 1:18, 1 Tim. 1:17, 6:16, etc., but point a Hindu to these profound truths and to our need to bow before God and His word.

7. *Share your testimony,* describing your personal experience of lostness and God's gracious forgiveness and peace. Don't claim to know God in His majesty and fullness, but share what you know in your life and experience. This is the supreme approach in presenting Christ to the Hindu, but care must be taken that our sharing is appropriate. To shout on a street corner or share at every seeming opportunity is offensive. What God does in our lives is holy and private, only to be shared in intimacy with those who will respect the things of God and His work in our lives.

8. *Lead in prayer and worship together with your Hindu friend.* Hinduism has a grand tradition of deep spirituality, and so it is

only by deeply spiritual means that we can expect to bring Hindus to the feet of Jesus Christ. Worship in spirit and truth and communion with God in prayer will open our Hindu friends to the riches of the spirituality available to the followers of Christ. This is the atmosphere most conducive to the Holy Spirit's work of bringing Hindus into discipleship to Jesus.

A Hindu who professes faith in Christ must be helped as far as possible to work out the meaning of that commitment in his own cultural context. Often a new follower of Christ is ready to adopt any and every practice of Western Christians, and needs to be taught what is essential and what is secondary in Western Christian life and worship. For example, it can be shown that the eastern practice of removing shoes in a place of worship has strong Biblical precedence despite the fact that shoes are worn in Western churches.

A new believer should be warned against making an abrupt announcement to his or her family, since that causes great pain and inevitably produces deep misunderstanding. Ideally, a Hindu will share each step of the pilgrimage to Christ with his or her family, so that there is no surprise at the end. An early stage of the communication, to be reaffirmed continually, would be the honest esteem for Indian/Hindu traditions in general that the disciple of Christ can and does maintain.

Approaching Hindus on these lines does not result in quick conversions and impressive statistics. But a hearing will be gained from some who have refused to listen to traditional Christian approaches. And new disciples of Christ can be taught to deal more sensitively with their contexts, allowing them to maintain an ongoing witness to their family and society. As the leaven of the gospel is allowed to work in Hindu society the living Christ will draw people to Himself.

recommended reading

On Hinduism

A Survey of Hinduism by Klaus K. Klostermaier (State University of New York Press, Albany, 1989) gives a masterful overview touching every aspect of the classical Hindu tradition, with frequent illustrations related to present day situations as well.

Hindus: Their Religious Beliefs and Practices by Julius Lipner (Routledge, New York, 1992) gives a carefully balanced presentation, full of information yet aiming to give a feel for Hindu perspectives rather than merely a set of facts.

The Camphor Flame: Popular Hinduism and Society in India by C. J. Fuller (Princeton University Press, 1992) helpfully surveys Hinduism in its more practical aspects, such as worship, rituals, festivals, and pilgrimage. Here one gets a true taste of Hindu life.

Understanding Hinduism by Dayanand Bharati (Munshiram Manoharlal, 2005). A general introduction to all aspects of Hinduism, but with a focus on the average Hindu practitioner and his/her perspectives and problems.

On Christ in the Hindu World

Exploring the Depths of the Mystery of Christ: K. Subba Rao's Eclectic Praxis of Hindu Discipleship to Jesus by H. L. Richard (Centre for Contemporary Christianity, Bangalore, 2005) introduces a remarkable Hindu disciple of Jesus, situating him in relation to

Hinduism and the church in India, with an analysis of lessons to be learned from sociological identification and theological syncretism.

Following Jesus in the Hindu Context: The Intriguing Implications of N. V. Tilak's Life and Thought by H. L. Richard (William Carey Library, 1998) tells the story of the greatest of Protestant pioneers in Hindu contexts, establishing the fundamentals of what contextual ministry among Hindus means.

Living Water and Indian Bowl: An Analysis of Christian Failings in Communicating Christ to Hindus, with Suggestions Toward Improvements (ISPCK, 1997 rev. ed. 2001) gives a practitioner's account of contextual ministry and the imperative need to move on from traditional to contextual ministry approaches.

Faith Meets Faith: Some Christian Attitudes to Hinduism in the Nineteenth and Twentieth Centuries by Eric J. Sharpe (SCM Press, London, 1977) is not an evangelical study but gives a very interesting and helpful overview of attitudes in mission history, right up to the dialogue movement of today.

New Patterns for Discipling Hindus by B. V. Subbamma (William Carey Library, Pasadena, 1970) contains helpful pointers toward an appropriate missionary strategy.

R. C. Das: Evangelical Prophet for Contextual Christianity edited by H. L. Richard (ISPCK, Delhi, 1993) gives a clear picture of the challenge involved in and the steps that need to be taken for effective work among Hindus.

glossary of important hindu terms

āchārya – Spiritual or religious teacher, often the head of an ashram.

advaita – Non-dualism or monism; the Vedantic philosophical school that sees all reality as one, especially emphasizing the Upanishadic teaching that the human soul (*ātman*) is not essentially different from the universal soul (*brahman*).

āgama – tradition, but particularly established non-Vedic traditions that dominate the practices of most Hindu *sampradāyas*.

ahimsā – Non-violence.

Alvars – South Indian (Tamil) *bhakti* poets who were devoted to the god Vishnu in his various manifestations.

ānanda – Bliss, joy.

anubhāva – Experience; considered the ultimate determinant of truth by some Hindus.

Aranyakas – Vedic writings often considered part of the Upanishads.

ārati – Worship through the waving of lamps in a clockwise circular motion before a deity.

Arjuna – Central figure in the Bhagavad Gita; Krishna is his charioteer.

artha – Productivity; one of the four purposes of life (*purushārthas*).

Arya Samaj – A nineteenth century reform group which called Hindus back to the Vedas, opposing caste and idolatry.

Aryan – The Sanskrit term means "noble"; later racial connotations to the term are of debatable validity. That the Aryans migrated into India a few millennia before Christ is still generally accepted, although highly disputed by most Hindutva votaries.

āshram – 1. A retreat center; traditionally a hermitage for ascetics. 2. A stage in the life of a high caste Hindu (see *sannyāsa*).

Asoka – Ancient (third century BC) ruler of India who converted to Buddhism and did much to spread the Buddhist faith beyond India.

Atharva Veda – The fourth and last Veda, containing many magic spells and the beginnings of Ayurvedic medicine.

ātman – Usually translated soul or self, but often very different from the biblical concept of soul. In many cases the term refers to "God considered as immanent in human personality."

aum – See *om*.

avatāra – Divine descent or incarnation; a fundamental belief of Vaishnava Hindus, rooted in the Bhagavad Gita (although the term itself is not used there).

Ayurveda – The science of health, or ancient Indian medical science. Many texts and traditions contributed to the development of Ayurvedic medicine.

Bhāgavad Gita – A section of the Mahabharata epic, often printed separately and esteemed as the greatest Hindu scripture. Dated between 200 BC and AD 200.

bhagavān – God, particularly the object of *bhakti*; the blessed or glorious one.

bhajan – A spiritual song, usually sung antiphonally and repetitiously.

bhakta – A devotee.

bhakti – Devotion. (The most popular of the traditional three ways to attain salvation.)

Bhārata – Traditional name for India in Sanskrit.

Brahmā – A personal manifestation of the universal soul, especially known as the creator.

Brahma Sutras – Aphoristic text which is the basis for Vedanta philosophy; also referred to as the Vedanta Sutras.

brahmacharya – The first stage of life when a boy goes to study under a guru.

brahman – The universal soul or essence of all things (sometimes spelled *brahma* or *brahm*).

Brahman – The first of the four *varnas*, or the highest of the castes of Hinduism, traditionally priests (often spelled Brahmin).

Brahmo Samaj – A nineteenth century reform group that promoted Vedic theism and held Christ in high esteem.

buddhi – The higher mind; reason; soul (many shades of meaning).

caste – A social division mentioned in the Vedas that at later stages developed into a rigid hierarchy based on birth. Two Sanskrit terms are translated as caste though their meanings are quite different. There are four castes (Sanskrit *varna*) of Brahman (priestly castes), Kshatriya (soldier castes), Vaisya (merchant castes), and Sudra (menial working castes). Many not even ranking as Sudras were considered outcastes (Dalits). In practical outworking castes (Sanskrit *jāti*) are innumerable; this practical meaning of caste is basically the endogamous unit, and the hierarchy of *jātis* is contested everywhere.

Chaitanya – A devotee of Krishna who spearheaded a *bhakti* revival in Bengal in the early sixteenth century.

cit – Consciousness (pronounced and sometimes written as *chit*).

Dalits – The oppressed; traditionally known as untouchables or outcastes or *hārijans* or *pānchamas*, in government terminology the Scheduled Castes. Nearly twenty percent of India's population; in some definitions the tribal peoples of India are also included.

darshan – Visual contact with a source of spiritual inspiration, particularly an image of a deity.

dharma – Duty, righteousness, order, that which sustains society, etc.

dikshā – A rite of initiation or dedication, particularly to a guru.

Dipavali or Divali – The festival of lights, largest of the national religious holidays among Hindus, celebrated over five days in recognition of various gods and goddesses.

Dravidian – The name of a family of south Indian (mostly) languages, often wrongly used as a racial term in opposition to Aryan.

Durga – The mother goddess, particularly as slayer of demonic forces; see Kali, *shakti*.

dvija – Twice-born, in reference to the *upanāyana* ceremony where a high caste male is invested with the sacred thread.

Ganesha – The elephant-headed son of Shiva who is the remover of obstacles, and so highly honored as a prosperity god. Also known as Vinayaka or Ganapati.

Ganga – The Ganges River, the most sacred of India's many holy rivers.

gāyatri mantra – A sacred chant recited daily by devout Brahmans; a prayer to the sun or to God as represented by the sun.

guna – Constituents of created reality; goodness (*sattva*), passion (*rajas*) and darkness (*tamas*) are the three *gunas*.

guru – A teacher, in the highest spiritual sense often considered and treated as a god.

Hanuman – The monkey god, Ram's loyal devotee.

Hindutva – "Hindu-ness;" a twentieth century movement to promote Hindu nationalism, or the traditional Hindu way, often noted for strong resistance to Islam and Christianity in India.

Holi – Festival of colors celebrated every spring.

Jainism – Ancient faith that developed with Buddhism as a severely other-worldly faith.

jāti – See caste.

ishta devatā – "Chosen deity;" eclectic Hindu traditions allow an individual to follow any of the deities to whom they might be particularly inclined.

jāñna – Knowledge; spiritual insight, especially as procured by meditation. (One of the three traditional ways to attain salvation.)

jāñni – One who practices and achieves *jāñna*.

Kabir – North Indian *bhakti* poet whose songs and sayings are widely known, traditionally thought to have been a Muslim weaver before his ascension as a spiritual leader.

Kali – One of numerous names for the mother goddess, she is also closely associated with Shiva; see Durga, *shakti*.

kāma – Desire (or lust; *kāmakrodha*, desire-anger, is shorthand for sin). In a more positive sense, "pleasure," one of the four purposes of life (*purushārthas*).

karma – 1. In the general sense, good works; religious, moral and caste duties. (One of the three traditional ways to attain salvation.) 2. The principle that reward or punishment infallibly follows every deed. At times the recompense comes in the present life; always the situation and fate of the coming life are determined by one's *karma*. (Often presented as an invariable law or as an expression of fatalism, but in fact there are multiple ways to affect and even manipulate *karma*.)

kirtan – A song or song service, often including teaching; various shades of meaning in various regions and traditions.

Krishna – An *avatāra* of Vishnu, or appearance of the supreme God on earth; supreme teacher in the Bhagavad Gita, celebrated focus of worship in various Puranas.

krodha – Anger (*kāmakrodha*, desire-anger, is shorthand for sin).

Kshatriya – The second of the four *varnas*; a group of high castes, traditionally the rulers and warriors of India.

Lingayats – A south Indian *sampradāya* which worships Shiva (also known as Virasaivism). Now a caste group more than the theological movement it once was; the dominant caste in Karnataka state.

lobha – Greed (often linked with *kāmakrodha*).

Mahābhārata – The great epic poem of India, consisting of 110,000 couplets. Broadly about a story of civil war in north India, but touching into every aspect of life. Traditionally authorship is ascribed to Vyasa, but clearly the epic developed and grew under many hands, generally dated between 400 BC to AD 400.

mahātma – Literally, great (*mahā*) soul (*ātma*).

manas – The mind which controls the senses (see *buddhi*); soul (many shades of meaning).

mandir – Temple.

mantra – Technically a verse of Vedic scripture, but popularly a word or saying of mystic meaning considered to have great power.

mārga – Path, or particularly way of salvation, especially *jāñna mārga* or the way of knowledge, *karma mārga* or the way of works and *bhakti mārga* or the way of devotion.

māyā – "Illusion" in some philosophical contexts; "creative power" in the Bhagavad Gita.

Mirabai – A *bhakti* poetess famed for her devotion to Krishna.

moksha – Release, salvation.

mukti – Salvation.

Murugan – A son of Shiva, a very popular god among the Tamils.

math – Monastery or ashram.

Nanak – North Indian *bhakti* poet whose tradition developed into the Sikh religion.

Narayan – One of many names of the god Vishnu, who incarnated himself primarily as Ram and Krishna.

Nayanars – South Indian (Tamil) poets devoted to the god Shiva.

nishkāma – Without desire (for fruit or reward, in the philosophical phrase *nishkāma karma*).

om – A mystic syllable without definition, often used in meditation and at the beginning and ending of any spiritual writing or service.

Outcastes – See Dalits.

pandit – A scholar or learned man, but often used indiscriminately of Brahmans.

prasād – 1. Grace. 2. Consecrated food that has been offered to a deity.

pujā – Worship.

pujāri – Priest who conducts ritual worship.

Purānas – Late (AD 600 to 1600) Sanskrit scriptures containing innumerable myths and legends, some of which are ancient. Eighteen major and eighteen minor Puranas are traditionally referred to, but there is no agreed classification of these works.

purusha – Literally "man." Used philosophically in the Bhagavad Gita as the opposite of *prakriti*, which is the contingent order; thus *purusha* is the eternal divine principle that transcends contingent reality in the Gita and in Samkhya philosophy.

Purusha Sukta – Rig Veda 10:90, a creation hymn wherein the cosmic man (*purusha*) is dismembered in a sacrificial ritual resulting in the creation of the universe, including the four-fold caste (*varna*) system.

purushārthas – The four purposes of life; *kāma* (pleasure), *artha* (productivity), *dharma* (duty or righteousness, which defines boundaries for *kāma* and *artha*) and *moksha* (salvation, the supreme aim of life).

Ram – Hero of the Ramayana, apparently a historical figure who grew into popular recognition as an incarnation (*avatāra*) of the god Vishnu.

Ramananda – The *bhakti* saint considered the primary agent for the spread of *bhakti* movements from south to north India.

Ramanuja – Eleventh century AD *visishtādvaita* Vedanta philosopher; proponent of theistic *bhakti*, the dominant philosophical tradition in Indian history.

Rāmāyana – Epic poem telling of Ram and his wife Sita. Valmiki was the original author around 300 BC. The myth developed over later centuries and the retelling by Tulsidas (the sixteenth century AD *Rāmcharitmānas*) is more widely known and esteemed in north India than Valmiki's original. Reinterpretations (especially orally) continue to the present time.

reincarnation – *Punarjanma* or *karma samsāra* – teaching rooted in the Upanishads, that new births on earth occur for beings who during their lifetime fail to attain salvation.

rishi – Sage; a patriarch possessed of great power and/or wisdom.

RSS – Rashtriya Swayamsevak Sangh, national self-service organization; mother movement for various Hindutva organizations.

saccidānanda – Truth/reality/being (sat), consciousness (cit), bliss (*ānanda*); the highest designation for the Supreme Being in Vedantic thought.

sadguru – The true guru ("*sat guru*").

sādhana – Spiritual discipline.

sādhu – A broad term for an ascetic or holy man.

Sai Baba – A series of modern gurus claim this title/name. Shirdi Sai Baba was probably born a Muslim; his foundational shrine is in rural Maharashtra and he is widely acknowledged in Mumbai and Maharashtra. Satya Sai Baba (b. 1926) of Puttaparthi (Andhra Pradesh) is the most widely followed guru in India today.

Saivism – Hindu traditions focused on Shiva as the supreme God.

sampradāya – Literally, tradition. A religious order or sect or "denomination" among Hindus.

samsāra – Generally, the world; in philosophical contexts, the cycle of reincarnations (as in *karma samsāra*).

samskāra – Sacraments or life cycle rituals, of which sixteen are generally listed, with many fewer in practice by most Hindus; marriage and death ceremonies are the most significant.

sanātana dharma – "Eternal way of life," a designation for Hinduism that is favored by many Hindus.

Samkhya – One of the six schools of Hindu philosophy, but a term which in the Bhagavad Gita means a philosophically reflective knowledge-system.

sannyāsa – Renunciation. Traditionally the fourth and last stage of life (*āshrama*) for a high caste Hindu, the others being *brahmacharya* (student), *grihasthya* (householder or family man), and *vānaprasthya* (recluse for meditation). In *sannyāsa* everything is renounced, including family, caste status and worship of idols. This is final preparation for death, breaking all earthly bonds in advance. Rarely was this ideal of a four-stage life practiced.

sannyāsi – Technically, one in *sannyāsa*, but often the term is used more loosely like *sādhu*.

Sanskrit – Language of the Hindu scriptures, still spoken by some *pandits*.

sāstras – A general term for various Hindu religious books.

sat – Existence, reality, truth.

satsang – A gathering focused on truth or reality.

satyāgraha – Gandhi's name for his non-violent resistance movement aimed at winning over a foe by enduring undeserved suffering, which he applied against the British Raj.

sevā – Service.

shakti – Power, but also a generic name for the mother goddess.

Shankara – The most famous exponent of *advaita* Vedanta philosophy; founder of monasteries that continue to this day; his name having become the title for the monastery heads; so the original Shankara (eighth century AD) is commonly designated Âdi (i.e. first)-Shankara, or *ādishankarāchārya* (the esteemed teacher, first Shankara).

shānti – Peace.

Sikhism – A *bhakti* religion from the sixteenth century AD which looks to Guru Nanak as founder and the Granth Sahib as scripture; the dominant faith in Punjab state.

Sita – Wife of Ram, the epitome of feminine virtue.

Shiva – Supreme God to many Hindus; an erotic ascetic in many myths of his creative and destructive power.

Sudra – The fourth caste; traditionally not permitted to know the higher teachings of Hinduism or even to enter the temples of the higher castes. Roughly equivalent to the modern government term of "other backward castes" (OBCs), numbering roughly half the population of India.

swāmi – A spiritual leader, but often just a title for a respected guru.

tathāstu – So let it be; amen.

Tukaram – Generally acknowledged as the greatest of the Marathi Hindu poet-saints, born around 1608 and died (by tradition was taken bodily up to heaven) in 1649.

untouchables – See Dalits.

Upanishads – A collection of mystical and philosophical writings. One hundred and eight are traditionally recognized, but thirteen are generally held to be the oldest and most authoritative. These are the end of the Vedic canon, or the *Vedānta*.

Vaisya – The third of the four *varnas* (see caste), traditionally businessmen of various types.

Vaishnavism – Hindu traditions focused on Vishnu as the supreme God.

varna – See caste.

Veda – The most ancient of Hindu scriptures. In the broader meaning the Vedas are Hymns (often referred to as Vedas in the more narrow meaning), the *Brāhmanas* (mainly rituals and *mantras* for the priests (Brahmans)), and the Upanishads.

Vedangas – The "limbs" of the Vedas; ritualism, astronomy, phonetics, prosody, etymology and grammar are the traditional branches of post-Vedic learning.

Vedānta – The dominant school of Indian philosophy, of which *advaita* is one sub-school. Literally means "end of the Vedas," taken to mean the culmination of the Vedas or as a reference to the Upanishads as the last section of the Vedas, from which the *Vedānta* philosophies are primarily developed.

Vedāntin – A follower of Vedanta philosophy.

Vishnu – Supreme God to most Hindus; noted for appearances on earth, particularly in ten different *avatāras*; usually worshipped in his manifestations as Ram and Krishna.

yoga – In general usage, deep contemplation or meditation. In more technical usage, one of various methods of physical discipline and meditation through which total self-control or God-realization are acquired. Also one of the six orthodox schools of Hindu philosophy.

yuga – Cosmic age, of which there are four; currently it is the *kali yuga*, the last and most degenerate.